THE NIC
TRA
and
HOW TO BEAT IT

A REVOLUTIONARY NEW APPROACH TO QUITTING SMOKING

Absolutely no cravings guaranteed!

Russell Board BSc

CONTENTS

CHAPTER 1

A BIT ABOUT ME

I started smoking when I was 13 and smoked for 10 years. I always knew that I shouldn't smoke but for some reason once I'd started, I just couldn't stop. Something overwhelmingly powerful had got hold of me and was refusing to let go! I found even thinking about stopping was something that I just would not do. I would just keep putting it off, there never seemed to be a right time. I'll do it tomorrow or next week or just sometime in the future, but not today!

Many of my friends at school were smokers and so it was something we would all do together. There was a real sense of comradery between us; we were all in it together. In fact, it was because of one of my friends that I started in the first place. He had an older sister who was a smoker and during the school holidays he'd given it a try and, of course, got hooked. He then persuaded me to try and because of my curious nature I decided to give it a go. It wasn't long before there was a group of us all happily smoking together.

No-one questioned it in the beginning, it was exciting. As far as we were concerned, we were exploring this 'adult only' experience and in the short term there was no question of stopping. Instead we would spend time looking for new places to smoke so that we wouldn't get caught. This, of course, was the downside of smoking at school. It was obviously not allowed and if you were caught there were severe punishments which increased in severity the more times you were caught.

It wasn't long before I'd been caught a few times and my parents were told and this was the start of many years of nagging from them to stop. The problem was I had no real understanding of what I was doing, and my parents didn't understand either; they had no idea that the nagging was never going to work. They didn't realise that I couldn't stop even if I wanted to and so the nagging just served to drive us further apart. I felt I was old enough to make those decisions myself and therefore refused to listen to any suggestion that I should stop.

Obviously, all my friends were getting grief from their parents too, so we were all in the same boat. Even so none of us ever talked about giving up. We all knew it was bad for us and that we shouldn't be doing it but that wasn't enough. We were enjoying our new-found independence and smoking was a big part of it. We were living for the now and giving up smoking was something that we would do when we were older, maybe, but certainly not now.

As I got older the novelty of smoking wore off and of course the relentless burden of funding the habit made me think that I should stop. Not that I wanted to stop; I can honestly say I never 'wanted' to stop. It was only because I knew it was so bad that I eventually came to the conclusion that I would try to stop.

The first time I tried to stop I seem to remember I lasted two days. To begin with it was easy as I had really psyched myself up, but I soon came unstuck after a game of cricket. I was walking back with a friend of mine; it was a beautiful summer evening and suddenly my friend declared that he was going to have a smoke and watch the sunset. Bang!

From nowhere this huge desire came over me to join him for a smoke. Until then I wasn't even thinking about it and was quite happy, but suddenly I was faced with this huge dilemma and of course I quickly crumbled as I imagined how good that smoke would be watching the sun set over the horizon on a perfect summer's eve. 'I'll give up another time', I thought.

Having found it quite easy to stop for 2 days I felt reassured that I could have the odd smoke no problem. Of course, that one cigarette was enough to get me back on it again. Immediately after it my resolve to stop smoking began to wane and I was soon back to smoking as much as before. I realised then that giving up was easy but staying stopped was the hard part!

In the following years I tried and failed many times to stop. Each time was the same method. I would psyche myself up for weeks beforehand and then one day just stop and see if I could stay stopped. The length of time I managed to stop for varied quite considerably from a single day up to a whole week. No matter how much I tried though I always ended up back on it; I just couldn't stay stopped for long. Life just wasn't the same without nicotine and at some point the withdrawal pangs would just be too much and I'd end up saying, 'what the hell,' and have a cigarette.

This all changed, however, when I undertook a degree in physiology at university. For those who do not know what physiology is, it is the science of how the body works. Everything from the circulatory system to cells communicating with each other on a molecular level.

For the first 2 years of the course I smoked more than ever but it was at the end of my second year that I made an amazing realisation about how nicotine actually works. I

4

then postulated that what was actually triggering the withdrawal pangs was totally preventable!

With my new-found knowledge I tried to stop smoking again. This time I knew what I was dealing with on a whole new level and I concentrated on what I thought might beat the cravings and as a result I developed a little technique for dealing with them and sure enough it actually worked. I couldn't believe it; I'd discovered a method for preventing the cravings and it meant I was able to get off nicotine no problem at all. It was totally mind blowing!

Once I had managed to get off nicotine properly it was as if I'd been in some sort of prison for 10 years and I was free again at last. It felt wonderful! It suddenly hit me how evil nicotine is for how it had taken over my life for so long. I was very emotional for a few weeks while my body and mind recovered. It really hit me hard that I had been addicted for so long.

If you can understand the drug the way I do then you will have no trouble becoming a very contented ex-consumer. And I really mean 'very contented'. You will never want to consume nicotine again and you will never be tempted. You will become how you were before you started, blissfully unaware that you should have anything to do with nicotine. If you fancy that read on!

CHAPTER 2

HOW THIS BOOK WILL WORK

IMPORTANT – From now on whenever you read this book make sure you stay topped up with nicotine. As I will explain a nicotine deprived brain does not think clearly and certainly will not entertain any ideas about giving it up. Believe me it is a very subtle beast!

My method will work for any kind of nicotine addiction whether it be smoking, vaping or chewing tobacco, it's all the same stuff. I therefore use the phrase 'nicotine consumption' throughout the book rather than smoking, vaping or chewing per se.

This book will describe to you a whole new approach to quitting nicotine. When you finish this book, you should be able to stop consuming nicotine any time you want and not experience any cravings whatsoever – I absolutely guarantee it!

This is because I have worked out exactly how we get caught in the nicotine trap and consequently have discovered a simple trick for preventing withdrawal symptoms/cravings from kicking in when we stop consuming nicotine.

Nicotine is not a drug you can take or leave. If you consume nicotine with any degree of repetition, even if it is just once a week, you are addicted to nicotine. You have been conned by the biggest scam the world has ever seen!

I will explain how the physical dependency can be overcome in just three days and teach you a trick that will make those three days easy to endure meaning you suffer no cravings whatsoever. At the same time though, I will explain how you have become psychologically addicted to nicotine and how, using my method, you can reverse the thing that drives this psychological dependency.

Nicotine itself is easy to give up once you know how, and if you only smoke once a week you are going through the physical withdrawal process each week without even noticing it. The reason you keep consuming it is because you have not addressed the psychological dependency. This is what keeps you coming back for more and I will teach you how to undo this so that you will never be caught out again.

If you follow my instructions properly you will not suffer one single craving. I will give you the tools you need to escape this all-consuming addiction once and for all. I therefore stress that for the book to work you must read the whole book. Don't be tempted to pick and choose bits to read. You must read it, in order, from the beginning right to the end. You must also understand everything I am telling you. If there is the tiniest thing you don't understand then you must re-read that section. You must understand how it works, that is the key to getting off this drug.

Everyone has a different level of education when it comes to science and to get off nicotine it is essential to understand the science of how this drug actually works. It is a very subtle beast and that is why the true mechanism of how it keeps you hooked has never been clearly understood until now. Through my own experience combined with my knowledge of how the body works on a molecular level, I have worked out exactly what is going on in the body when you try to stop consuming nicotine.

With this information I have worked out what you have to do to come off nicotine without any cravings. It is so simple you will not believe that is all it takes, but nicotine addiction depends solely on a programmed reaction kicking in once you stop consuming it. I will give you the key to stopping that reaction. Once you prevent the reaction from happening you will not even notice coming off nicotine. This is what all other methods fail to address and as I will explain, this reaction is the key to keeping you coming back for more.

In the next chapter I will explain how nicotine works and then in the chapter after that I will teach you a method of how to quit that is so easy you will be stunned. Once you learn my technique you will be amazed at how easy it can be to leave nicotine behind for good – I guarantee it!

CHAPTER 3

HOW NICOTINE WORKS – THE WORLD'S BIGGEST SCAM

Thinking about giving up nicotine can be a very scary proposition. Many consumers never even think about giving up as they just accept that they want that regular hit in their lives. It is always there ready to deal with any stressful situation calming you down and making you feel nice and comfortable. As a consumer you don't know why but when you go without it for a while you start to feel uncomfortable. Gradually you start thinking about consuming nicotine and how it would feel good to have a hit. The longer you go without it the more you think about it and the more uncomfortable you feel. Eventually you cannot stop thinking about consuming it to take away the uncomfortable feeling that has developed in your body.

The cravings, as they are called, become so strong that you will go right out of your way to get a fix. I remember many a time trekking to an all-night garage in the middle of the night to get a fix, and the longer you leave it the more uncomfortable you feel until eventually the desire to feel comfortable again is so strong you find yourself a hit. Once you've had your hit you feel good again for a while until gradually the whole process starts again.

It's a relentless process once you become hooked and it takes over your whole life. Your life revolves around nicotine consumption. You have accepted that it is just something that you do. Occasionally, but only occasionally, you might think you should stop, but something just keeps driving you on and on, so much so that thinking about stopping can just be a fleeting thought and actually acting on it becomes extremely rare.

Early on in your addiction you might have tried a few times to give up, but you quickly realise that it is so hard to just stop consuming. You just do not feel normal without it. Once you have tried and failed a few times you just convince yourself that it's ok to smoke or that you will give up sometime in the future.

The problem is the future comes and goes and even thinking about stopping becomes less and less frequent. You just accept that this is one of life's pleasures, no matter how bad, that you are going to pursue.

What if I told you that life on nicotine is actually an illusion? That actually the way you 'feel' all the time is nothing to do with the way nicotine acts on your body it's actually all to do with how your mind reacts to nicotine acting on your body.

Every nicotine consumer gets caught in the same trap and the trap is this:

Smoking is not 'really' pleasurable

Nicotine addiction is the biggest con on the planet. That is not an exaggeration. There is no 'high' from consuming it unlike other drugs which actually directly stimulate pleasure centres in our brain. Nicotine's high is created by ourselves over time.

'Smoking is pleasurable only for those who smoke'.

The pleasure that people get from smoking is not a genuine pleasure. There is no 'hit' when nicotine is first consumed. It actually only starts to become pleasurable once you have become addicted i.e. once you have consumed enough of it that your body goes through an uncomfortable withdrawal process. Only when nicotine is consumed again, the withdrawal symptoms are alleviated, that pleasure is perceived. The pleasure is genuine as you have become uncomfortable due to the process of withdrawal; consuming nicotine makes you feel comfortable again and it is this transition from being uncomfortable to being comfortable that can be very pleasurable.

That is the only hit nicotine gives you it's like relieving your bladder when you haven't been able to go for a while, like on a long car journey. You get used to the uncomfortable feeling building up but learn to endure it until you are able to stop at the service station. When you finally relieve yourself, the pleasure can be quite intense and you realise how uncomfortable you have actually been. Well that's a bit like nicotine addiction. When you stop consuming nicotine it's like letting your bladder fill up. The longer you go the more pleasure you will have when you eventually do go or consume nicotine again.

Do you now understand this most fundamental fact about nicotine addiction? You may well argue that this cannot be true but the fact is that all nicotine addicts have learnt over time that nicotine to them is pleasurable only because they have repeatedly become uncomfortable, and learned to associate the relieving of the uncomfortable feelings, i.e. pleasure, with nicotine consumption. It has become so entrenched in their psyche that they cannot see it for what it really is.

To begin with the withdrawal symptoms are very subtle and when everyone first tries nicotine they can take or leave it. This is how easy it really is to get off nicotine until the brain has become conditioned.

Think back to when you first tried nicotine. It was horrible right? Did you get high, did you get a pleasurable feeling and think wow this is really good I must do it again or did it make you feel sick and wonder why on earth do people do this?

This is the normal reaction to nicotine, if you did not have this reaction when you first tried it but instead found it pleasant then you must have been exposed to nicotine in your life sometime before either in the womb or you have lived in a house with smokers and you have unknowingly consumed nicotine so that it has altered the way you perceive it.

You must believe me that the natural reaction to nicotine is revulsion. The human body when first exposed to nicotine will not accept it. It is only after repeated exposure to it that our perception alters and it starts to taste and smell nice.

Nicotine has a huge effect on our bodies when we consume it. Every single muscle in your body has receptors on them that have been named by scientists as nicotinic receptors. Liken a receptor to a little switch which can only be activated by certain transmitter chemicals. In the body there are literally millions of receptors on the surfaces of millions of cells which make up every part of your body. There are also thousands of transmitter chemicals flowing between cells which activate different receptors on different cells. This is how the body's cells communicate with one another. It's extremely complicated and we won't got into too much detail here.

Scientists have called certain receptors on muscles nicotinic receptors because they have found that nicotine binds to and triggers these receptors. The body has its own transmitter chemicals that bind to and activate these receptors but when nicotine is present it binds to them and activates them in preference to the body's natural chemicals.

Nicotine actually mimics the natural transmitter molecules the body uses to cause muscles to relax. It must be remembered that even though the receptors on muscles are called nicotinic receptors, nicotine does not occur naturally in the body at all.

When you consume nicotine, therefore, all your muscle receptors are stimulated by nicotine. If this is the first time you've consumed nicotine your muscles will naturally be in a relaxed, 'normal,' state. The nicotine cannot cause any further relaxation as they are as relaxed as they can be but it does still latch onto the receptors and continues to stimulate them to relax.

If nicotine consumption is continued the body very quickly begins to recognise that it doesn't need to secrete as much of the normal transmitter molecules that keep the muscles relaxed as it normally does i.e. it adapts as nicotine is now doing the job keeping muscles relaxed.

However, when nicotine consumption is stopped the nicotine slowly begins to wash away from the muscle receptors, taking in actual fact 3 whole days to be fully washed away. As soon as the nicotine begins to be washed away, in response, the muscles very gradually begin to tense up. Because the body has adapted to the nicotine acting on the muscles it does not instantly begin secreting the natural transmitter chemicals that used to keep the muscles relaxed.

This is the start of the 'cravings' associated with stopping smoking. They are actually a physical feeling caused by every muscle in the body beginning to tense up.

When you first stop consuming nicotine this feeling is not that bad, as your body takes a while to adapt to the muscles being stimulated to relax with nicotine. The body's natural relaxation mechanism (NRM) only begins to switch off with prolonged nicotine exposure to the muscles i.e. you have to consume quite a lot of nicotine to fully shut down the NRM. Once it has been shut down though the body recognises nicotine as the new mechanism for keeping muscles relaxed and an association is now made in the brain i.e. it has become conditioned so that when your muscles tense up your brain demands nicotine to release the tension.

In the early days of nicotine consumption, you can take or leave it much easier as your bodies NRM is still active; your body has a memory of this system and brings it back into service. You have some success in giving up nicotine the first few times you try even though you always fall back into the trap. It's only over long periods of time that trying to stop becomes harder and harder due to the NRM becoming so inactive the body loses any memory of it, i.e. it fully adapts to the nicotine replacement system i.e. you consuming nicotine at regular intervals.

This is why the longer you consume nicotine the harder it becomes to give up, as even if you manage to get through the withdrawal stage your body is left in a constant state of tension, which as I will explain will have other major consequences even if you can endure it.

This is how the belief is born in your mind that nicotine actually relaxes you. It does, but only because it has made you tense in the first place.

Once shut down the NRM takes some prompting to start it up again and this is where most people go wrong as they fail to address this.

This is how you become dependent on nicotine. Even if you consume just one dose of nicotine all your muscle receptors will be stimulated by the nicotine and it will take 3 whole days for the nicotine to be fully washed away. That is a physiological fact and unavoidable. In that time, if you have been a regular consumer, all the muscles in your body will begin to tense up, not long after you had your last dose.

The longer you have been consuming for the quicker your muscles will begin to tense up as they steadily become de-sensitised to the nicotine i.e. it requires more and more nicotine to get the muscles to fully relax. It therefore goes that if you limit yourself to a set number of doses each day then you will steadily get more and more withdrawn i.e. 'tensed up' between doses as time goes by. This means that the hit you get from stopping the withdrawal 'pain' will become more and more pronounced reassuring you in your ill-found belief that nicotine consumption really is pleasurable.

Consuming nicotine is not at all pleasurable once you have got off the drug and it only takes 3 days to get off nicotine if you understand the withdrawal process and use my method. You must fully understand what is happening during the withdrawal process to stand any chance of long-term success.

CHAPTER 4

THE CONDITIONED NICOTINE RESPONSE (CNR)

The Conditioned Nicotine Response (CNR) is a term that I have coined. The term 'Conditioned Response' is a scientific term used to describe a learned change in behaviour as a result of an external stimulus that previously produced no response.

I apologise if that all sounds a bit scientific but it's essential that you understand this bit of science so please read on.

The scientist who discovered this phenomenon was a Russian physiologist called Ivan Pavlov. He was studying salivation in dogs and how they would start to salivate when food was placed in front of them. During the course of these experiments, however, he made an observation that the dogs would begin to salivate when they heard the footsteps of the person bringing the food. This was obviously well before the food was placed in front of them. Food being placed in front of a dog will always produce the salivation reaction as it is an instinctive reaction needed to help the dogs actually consume the food. This is therefore not a learned behaviour.

Pavlov realised that the dogs were making a subconscious association between the sound of footsteps and the arrival of food. Because they were learning that they would get food shortly after hearing the footsteps, the footsteps on their own were now causing the dogs to salivate before the food was actually placed in front of them. He therefore reasoned that the dogs had learned or become 'conditioned' to the sound of the footsteps and with them consequently being fed.

He then decided to see if the dogs could be 'conditioned' (learn) to respond (salivate) to other stimuli, so he started introducing the sound of a metronome just before presenting food and the same thing occurred. After a few occasions of playing the metronome before feeding, the dogs learned that the sound of the metronome meant they were going to be fed and so began to salivate   After much repetition the dogs would salivate whenever they heard the sound of the metronome on its own, even if food wasn't presented to them immediately afterwards. The metronome sound alone was enough to illicit a response. The response had been subconsciously learned by the dogs.

This set of experiments led to what is now called Classical Conditioning or Pavlovian Conditioning. It is the brain learning to respond to a stimulus which on its own previously did not cause any response. If we go back to the footsteps of the dog feeder the footsteps previously on their own did not cause the dogs to salivate. It was only after being fed immediately afterwards a few times did the dog's brains make the association with the fact that food wasn't far away.

Any dog owner will recognise this happens quite a lot with dogs especially when it comes to going for a walk. Dogs will become excited when they see you putting on your hat and coat and picking up the dog lead or hearing you open a tin of dog food. Cats also demonstrate this, they especially love the sound of tins being opened, I remember my cat would be constantly brushing up against me, purring like crazy and meowing as I prepared the cat food on the bench.

You might be thinking how can this be related to nicotine addiction? Well it is the most fundamental part of why nicotine is so hard to give up, or so hard to give up if you don't know about it and deal with it!

I made a realisation, through my own observations, when quitting nicotine based on my knowledge of physiology/psychology and the conditioned response that as soon as my muscles began to tense up my brain triggered a response for me to consume nicotine. The response for me is very difficult to describe but only that it would involve me gradually becoming stressed. It would eventually result in an extremely agitated state of mind which would always result in me thinking about consuming nicotine.

I'm sure you all know what I mean as this is what drives us all to keep consuming. My realisation that there was a conditioned response going on came when I noticed that if I made a conscious effort to keep my muscles relaxed there would be no resulting panic in my brain leading to me eventually starting to think about nicotine. With practice I learned to anticipate my muscles becoming tense during the withdrawal process and as long as I addressed this, I would not think about consuming nicotine at all. Suddenly getting off nicotine became really easy!

As soon as the nicotine consumption is stopped your muscles will begin to tense up. We don't really notice that this is happening but I can assure you this is definitely happening to every single nicotine addict the world over every time they stop consuming nicotine and it starts happening almost immediately after a dose. It is absolutely unavoidable. It is the muscles adjusting to the nicotine washing away from their receptors.

Most addicts don't notice this to begin with. They just 'feel' this as starting to feel uncomfortable and eventually the longer they go the more uncomfortable they feel. But what is actually happening in their bodies is that every single muscle, large and small, all over their bodies is beginning to tense up. Very slowly to begin with but gradually more and more as time goes by.

This is the same reaction when we become stressed, our muscles tense up. We even describe being stressed as being 'tense'. Yes, we physically, our muscles, have become tense.

When you are addicted to nicotine, over time, a conditioned response has developed that when your muscles tense up your brain demands nicotine to make them relax. This is the crux of why smoking is so difficult to stop. When the brain demands nicotine for some people this can be a mild demand, but for most addicts this eventually leads to absolute panic and the beginning of an extremely stressed out state of mind. Yes, the body is tense, and this is uncomfortable for most people but how this then affects the mind can vary considerably from person to person, which is why some people become more easily addicted than others.

This is where the main confusion with nicotine addiction lies. It is this conditioned response to the muscles tensing that can lead to very different reactions in different people. For most people who have been smoking a long time the panic response is the more usual and the longer the muscles go without being relaxed the more this panic can develop. If you are not good generally at dealing with stress, (and who is?), then this can quickly lead to a very agitated state of mind.

This is why most people find it so hard to stop as it is the stressed-out mind that they simply can't deal with, which for all addicts just gets worse the longer they go without nicotine. The simplest things in life can become very stressful and life becomes one stressful event after another. The brain gets stuck in this pattern of behaviour and it's not long before they are a nervous wreck. It's then just a matter of time before they turn back to the nicotine sanctuary from which they've come, usually when their guard is down after having a drink or an especially stressful day/event.

As soon as nicotine is consumed the muscles become relaxed and as soon as the muscles are in a relaxed state the conditioned response stops being triggered, with the resulting panic in the brain stopping. If a big panic has developed and you have become very uncomfortable the feeling of reliving that uncomfortable state can be absolute bliss. Every nicotine addict knows that feeling which is why they confuse it with nicotine actually giving them a hit. There is no real hit, you've only made yourself comfortable from being extremely uncomfortable in your body and in your mind.

As your muscles relax the response of the brain is to stop consuming nicotine, which is why you stop thinking about getting a fix once you've just had one. Immediately after a dose of nicotine is the only time in an addict's life when the brain actually functions normally. Once you have had enough nicotine it really does not do anything anymore and starts to become unpleasant which is why you stop consuming. This is the normal brains reaction to nicotine. Once you've had a dose you think normally for a short time and I'm sure, if you think about it, you will agree that the appeal of nicotine has totally gone, which is why you stop consuming it. It begins to taste unpleasant and if you keep consuming eventually starts to taste pretty horrible. Of course, all addicts stop consuming as soon as they reach that 'normal' state and will never usually continue beyond that.

Hopefully you now understand what a conditioned response is and how this is the driving force behind your addiction. If you don't understand please re-read this chapter until you do, it's really important you understand this.

CHAPTER 5

HOW TO QUIT

To successfully quit nicotine you need to focus on the CNR. Period!

As you have hopefully now learnt, nicotine addiction revolves around the conditioned response or CNR as I call it. This is a learned response to consume nicotine as a result of the physical state of your muscles, as they adjust, after being stimulated by nicotine. Once nicotine is consumed, the conditioned response stops being triggered, resulting in the brain stopping its demand for consuming nicotine.

The conditioned response, as I have explained, is a learned response and as such it can be unlearned. Going back to Pavlov and his dogs, he wondered if it was possible to unlearn the association of the sound of the metronome with the dogs being fed and sure enough, he showed that this was possible. After being subjected to the stimuli but not being fed afterwards it didn't take long for the dogs to stop associating being fed with the sound of the metronome. They had unlearned the association. This is true with any conditioned response which therefore means it is possible to unlearn the CNR.

This is very important: There is only one way to get off nicotine properly and that is to just stop consuming it altogether. You cannot quit nicotine if you keep consuming it, no matter how small the amounts are. To successfully escape this drug and get back to being normal you must fully stop taking nicotine. You cannot wean yourself off this drug as your body needs the shock of having no nicotine in it to begin the process of unlearning the conditioned response; and if you don't unlearn the conditioned response you will always be vulnerable.

Do not believe anything you have read that says you can wean yourself off this drug with patches or cutting down or whatever! It's just physiologically impossible due to the fact that a conditioned response is involved. There's no getting away from that, we are all made exactly the same way and function physiologically exactly the same in that respect.

Imagine Pavlov's dogs only being given a small amount of food after hearing the stimuli, they are still going to have the association of food and the stimuli. How is that ever going to go away if you still keep presenting food? Likewise, unless you totally stop consuming nicotine and completely get it all out of your body you will not begin to unlearn the CNR. If you don't unlearn the CNR you will always be vulnerable to your brain demanding nicotine at some point in time if you ever become 'tense', which as we know can happen often in our hectic lifestyles. This is why many people who manage to quit for a while end up back on it, because they haven't dealt with the fundamental conditioning that has taken place i.e. the psychological dependency.

My method of quitting nicotine uses the CNR to ensure you do not have any withdrawal symptoms or cravings at all! As I've already told you, withdrawal from the drug causes the muscles to tense up and the muscles tensing up triggers the CNR in your brain to start panicking so that you will consume nicotine so as to relax the muscles. The secret therefore is to keep the muscles relaxed. If your muscles do not tense up then there will be no conditioned response by your brain to start panicking, resulting in you consuming nicotine.

It's as simple as that! All you need to do is stop your muscles from tensing up and you will not experience withdrawal symptoms I absolutely guarantee it! It's an inescapable physiological fact.

Imagine there's a switch in your brain that is triggered when your muscles begin to tense up. Once the switch has been triggered the brain goes into overdrive trying to get you to consume nicotine. Once you have consumed nicotine the switch is triggered again telling your brain to stop the demand for nicotine. Once you've had a dose of nicotine you don't want it any more right? Immediately after finishing a dose of nicotine you stop thinking about consuming nicotine don't you? That's because the switch has been activated in your brain that says you have got an acceptable level of nicotine in your body. This switch is driven by the tension in our muscles. By keeping your muscles relaxed the switch is not triggered. This is how nicotine works and this is it's Achille's heal. If you can prevent the switch from being triggered the brain thinks that you have consumed nicotine and you will not therefore think about wanting nicotine.

It is beautifully simple. Because all our bodies work the same way, I know this will work for everyone. What you need to do, therefore, is to learn how to relax your muscles again by yourself and this has got to be the focus if you want to escape from this drug. You cannot simply give up nicotine and expect your body to naturally relax your muscles again. You need to help your body 'remember' how to relax your muscles and you must do this as soon as you stop consuming nicotine. You need to prevent the muscles from tensing up.

This is all you need to do. If you can keep them relaxed you will never want nicotine again. Keeping your muscles relaxed mimics the physiological state that your body is in after it has had a full dose of nicotine and the point at which the CNR stops being triggered and your brain stops demanding nicotine. You are therefore unlearning the response or reversing the con.

No other method for giving up nicotine addresses this simple physiological fact. If you don't address this, once your muscles start to tense up through lack of the drug the CNR switch is constantly triggered. This is why it is so hard to just stop taking nicotine because nicotine addicts have lost the natural ability to relax the muscles and as soon as they stop consuming nicotine their muscles begin to tense up. Once your muscles become tense it is then extremely difficult to get away from nicotine when your brain is constantly telling you to consume it.

By actively concentrating on keeping your muscles relaxed you are ensuring the CNR is not being triggered as if you have just had a dose of nicotine. I promise you if you stay relaxed then you will not want another dose of nicotine during the withdrawal period. This will last three days and once you are through that it will only take two more days for you to fully recondition your brain back to normal. In five days you will be free from nicotine for ever and I guarantee you will not want to consume it ever again!

Once you get back to normal you see it for what it really is, a total con trick which has conned you every day for however long you've been a consumer. For me it was ten years of my life and when I finally broke free I felt like I'd just come out of prison. I have never been to prison but suddenly I felt free again. It was an amazingly emotional experience which brought me to tears regularly for a few days as I came to terms with the fact that I had been a slave to that drug every day for 10 years. I suddenly realised how every living moment of my life had revolved around making sure I was topped up with nicotine wherever I went and whatever I did. My nicotine level had rarely dipped and only a few times had I actually managed to stop consuming long enough to get it all out of my body only to be taken in by the con once more.

You are being physiologically conned, and you need to wake up and realise it! You must see it for what it really is.

All you need to do, to ride out the withdrawal process, which will only take three days, is to keep all your muscles relaxed. If you manage to do this, then you will not think about consuming nicotine. You will be normal again! Your brain will only demand nicotine if you let your muscles tense up.

As soon as you stop consuming nicotine your muscles start to tense up as the nicotine is washed away from the muscle receptors. This is very subtle to begin with but slowly but surely starts to become noticeable. Eventually a threshold is reached which triggers the CNR.

This is where people trying to give up always fail because they are just trying to ride out this tense state with the CNR being constantly triggered by tensed muscles. The brain is being constantly told it needs nicotine, muscles are tense. In this state of mind it is inevitably a losing battle. The problem, if you manage to get through this period, is it never really goes away. You must remind your body that its normal state is not to be tensed up. The danger, and it happens to so many people, is that you manage to get off nicotine, but because you have not 'reset' your muscles they are in a constant state of tension. This just results in a constantly agitated mind and a stressed-out person, who is then always vulnerable to going back to nicotine to 'relax' them, which of course it does. This just reinforces, in that person's mind, that nicotine actually helps you relax. It helps you relax because it got you tense in the first place!

I'm sure you all know people who have tried to give up smoking and how grumpy they can be when they first quit. This is because they are struggling to contain the panic that is ensuing in their minds. It is a constant battle in an addict's mind. It's like the most savage beast you can imagine that needs to be fed at regular intervals to stop it from becoming enraged. The hungrier it gets the more enraged it becomes until it's doing untold amounts of damage to get what it wants.

For the addict, nicotine withdrawal can result in some scary states of mind and due to the nature of the mind this varies enormously from person to person. One thing that is true for all, though, is that the longer they go without nicotine the more severe the symptoms become. Eventually the addict cannot stand it anymore and starts to consume again knowing that the symptoms will then go away.

With my method there will be no stressed-out state of mind. You will feel perfectly normal like you do when you have just finished having a dose of nicotine, but you have to focus on staying relaxed and this does take some effort. This is now what I need you to focus on as it must become your new vice if you want nicotine to be an old one.

CHAPTER 6

THE BREATH EXERCISE

This is the most important chapter of the whole book and the basis of my method. You must do this!

As I have already explained every muscle in your body is affected by nicotine and so every muscle reacts when you stop consuming nicotine by tensing up. This includes all the muscles associated with breathing. Every time you breath you are using lots of different muscle groups to raise and lower the chest. The main ones are called intercostal muscles and most of the time you don't even think about using them they are just working automatically, constantly lifting the chest up so as to expand the chest cavity so that air is pulled into the lungs.

For nicotine consumers these muscles are the most noticeable ones that tense up once you start withdrawing from nicotine, as they produce the so-called cravings associated with nicotine withdrawal; that physical feeling of the body yearning for nicotine. It starts in these muscles and once past a certain threshold the CNR is triggered that I have described before. As already mentioned, the CNR results in very different states of mind in different people based purely on their own way of dealing with stress.

Dealing with stress is something we all learn, or don't learn, primarily from our parents and from observing other humans around us and how they deal with situations in life. How many times have we seen the stressed out person in a movie come home from a hard day's work and pour himself a huge shot of Scotch. Not really the best way of dealing with a stressful day but how many of us do that? I guess someone meditating for 15 minutes would not be as interesting to watch. Also, I'm sure there's some subliminal advertising going on there that drinking is the way to deal with stress, but that's for another book!

Anyway, I'm getting off the subject here, the point is that we all deal with stress in different ways and so nicotine withdrawal can result in very different reactions amongst individuals. The key is to prevent yourself from becoming stressed and the way to do that is to prevent the CNR. Therefore, it's imperative that you do the following breath technique as a first step, as there is no other way of stretching out those intercostal muscles. This is something that you <u>must</u> do for my method to work. Stretching the intercostal muscles is the most important first step to prevent the CNR from kicking in. Stretching out these muscles is the best way to get them back to how they should be normally.

Sit down in a comfortable chair and then proceed to take three very deep breaths one after another. Take your time, each breath should be as deep as you can make it, really stretching those muscles that are lifting the chest as much as you can each time. On the final breath don't breathe out but hold it in your lungs for as long as you can until you feel a rush of oxygen to the brain. This oxygen rush to the brain may make you feel light-headed. This is perfectly normal and completely safe to do so don't worry about it just ride it out and you should begin to feel relaxed.

When you finally let that last breath out sit back in the chair and consciously try to relax all your muscles in your body at the same time. Try to melt into the chair, really focus on every muscle starting with your arms and working your way down your body to your feet. Focus your mind on each part of your body and 'let go' of the tension in each muscle.

This 'letting go' might seem a strange way of describing it but that's kind of what you have to do. For some people they never fully relax their muscles and so this is why I describe it as letting go. Really focus on a particular muscle group, for example the arms. Let them lie loosely by your sides and shut your eyes and focus on really trying to make them fully go limp and 'melt into the chair. Once you have got them to relax you may find this hard to maintain. They may twitch and insist on being tense. This is where you need to practice keeping them in this relaxed state. This is the key to quitting nicotine.

Wherever your mind is focused you should begin to tune into that area of your body and get the muscles to relax. Closing your eyes is therefore good at focusing on a certain area of your body and gradually move from one area to another until you have covered your whole body. Areas such as your neck and arms are important as these are close to your chest and have become associated with the feelings that are often called cravings. The cravings are just your muscles literally tightening up 'demanding' nicotine to relax them by triggering the CNR.

Hopefully after doing this you will feel relaxed. If you don't then do it all again until you do. Do not be afraid to repeat the breathing exercise. Once you have done this there should be no tightness in the lungs when you breath in, you should be able to take a nice satisfying deep breath. If you find you cannot take a nice deep breath, as if there's something constricting your chest, then this means your muscles are still a bit tensed up and you need to keep doing the breathing exercise, waiting a few minutes between each session so as not to hyperventilate. Really hold that last breath as long as you possibly can as it will really help with relaxing the whole body.

This is the crux of my method and if you don't manage to get your muscles to relax then my method will not work. As I've said over and over now it is the muscles tensing up that triggers the CNR and once that is triggered you are on the slippery slope that you know too well usually ends in you consuming nicotine, it'll be just a matter of time. It's therefore essential that you learn a little routine for de-tensing your muscles as they are going to keep tensing up over and over again throughout the withdrawal period.

As already mentioned, the majority of nicotine is out of your body after three days and completely out of your system in five. The tensing up of the muscles is very regular to begin with but gets less and less as you go through the withdrawal period. For the first day your muscles will tense up over and over again and you must keep on top of them. You may have to do the breath technique 3 or 4 times an hour if you were quite a heavy consumer. At the very least you should be doing it at the same times that you used to consume nicotine. Ideally before the time you would normally consume. If you wait too long, then the CNR will be triggered and you will struggle to get back under control. A nicotine deprived brain will quickly convince you that giving up was a bad idea and you could do it another time. You know the rest.

Learning to prevent your muscles tensing up is what you have to do. This is a whole new approach to quitting nicotine and is using the mechanism that actually keeps you on the drug against itself namely the CNR. As long as you prevent the CNR from being triggered you will not think about consuming nicotine and you will find it really easy to ride the three-day withdrawal period. This is how your brain has become wired with nicotine, if your muscles are tense then your brain thinks nicotine. Keep the muscles relaxed and the brain quite simply will not think about nicotine.

If you don't notice this tension developing you mustn't get complacent. We all have the same physiology and if you have consumed nicotine then you will go through a withdrawal period where your muscles will tense up, it is inevitable, it cannot be stopped. The thing is though this muscle tension can also be caused if we become stressed by a situation in life, for whatever reason. When we become stressed, we all have our own, mostly subconscious, methods of de-stressing. Some of us are much better at doing this than others and this is why it can be difficult recognising this nicotine tension as part of the withdrawal process.

Most consumers just think that this tension is normal and that's how nicotine use can be associated with being relaxing. How many times have you heard that as a reason for people consuming nicotine, because it relaxes them? Yes exactly, it relaxes you because you are becoming tense as you begin to withdraw from nicotine as a result of the effects of the nicotine on your muscles. When you then consume nicotine the muscles relax and this is pleasurable and so we make the association that nicotine is 'relaxing'. Nicotine is not relaxing, it is only relaxing once you have consumed it a few times i.e. once your muscles start to tense up.

Nicotine users therefore, due to the nature of their habit, are not very good at de-stressing naturally. They just rely on nicotine to relax them and this is the case even when they become tense for other reasons. It's therefore hard for consumers to recognise that they have to re-learn how to relax. They have been so used to letting nicotine do the job their natural mechanism has become redundant and doesn't kick in when required. This is why many ex-consumers are grumpy because they are in a constant state of stress.

This is another reason for focusing on de-stressing your muscles as you come off nicotine. If you quit nicotine without addressing this you run the risk of your muscles staying in a constant state of tension, which is reflected in a grumpy nature. You will not know why you feel grumpy but it will be because you are 'tense' and because you haven't re-learnt how to relax and you don't recognise that this is what it is.

This is one of the really evil aspects of nicotine addiction. It takes over and replaces our natural relaxation mechanism and makes it redundant. This then makes it really difficult to stay off it when you quit if you don't address this issue, and how many of us know to do that? Nicotine is easy to give up if you focus on staying relaxed. If you don't trigger the CNR you will not think about consuming nicotine. You will only ever think about consuming nicotine if the CNR is triggered, that's how it works. Stop the CNR from happening and you will not even notice the withdrawal process and before you know it you will be off the drug and back to normal and will never want to consume again!

On the morning of the first day it's very important to do the breath/relax technique as soon as you wake up. Then do it again at regular intervals of up to 10-15 mins depending on how you are feeling. Your body has already gone 8 hrs into the 72hrs needed to get off the drug and it will be starting to tense up as it is used to nicotine first thing every morning to do the job for it. You therefore need to be straight onto relaxing before the no-return switch is activated.

If you are relaxing properly you will not even think about having a dose of nicotine. If you can't stop thinking about nicotine you need to keep doing the relaxation technique. You have to learn to recognise that your muscles are tensed up and it will take some practice to tune into them again and keep them relaxed. Just keep trying!

If you find yourself at any time thinking about how nice it would be to have some nicotine, this means that you have become tense, usually in your chest. It's a feeling that you will be so used to tolerating and you may not even notice it as a result. The indicator that you are tense is the thought of wanting some nicotine. If you are not tense then you will not have the thought, the two are inextricably linked due to the CNR. This is why it is easy to quit nicotine as long as you actively keep your muscles relaxed. If you can't stop thinking about consuming nicotine then you need to do more to relax.

It may seem quite strange to begin with, actively trying to relax your muscles, but until you are through the five-day withdrawal period your mind will not unlearn the CNR. This is how long it takes and is unavoidable so you must actively attempt to get your muscles relaxed as they go through the withdrawal period and by doing so you will recondition your mind to keep the muscles relaxed without nicotine. You will feel normal again without nicotine!

CHAPTER 7

WHEN TO QUIT

Choosing the right time to quit is very important as you need to spend some time focusing on the relaxation techniques. For this reason, I would always recommend the weekend as the best time or better still take some holiday and get this thing done once and for all!

It will take a bit of practice to get all your muscles to relax and you must learn a little routine. This requires some effort and you must not be tempted to forego this. If you have been consuming nicotine for any length of time then your muscles will go through a period of withdrawal whether you like it or not. If you don't think that your muscles are tensing up when you stop consuming nicotine then you really need to sit or lie down and focus on them because there is no escaping the simple physiological fact that if you've consumed nicotine your muscles will begin to tense up once you stop consuming.

As I've mentioned before this is very subtle to begin with and most consumers would only eventually notice the chest muscles tensing up manifesting in the cravings that every consumer eventually gets. It's absolutely essential though that you stop the cravings from occurring. If you've let these muscles get this far the CNR will have already been triggered and you will undoubtedly be thinking of consuming nicotine. You must keep on top of the muscles tensing and do a regular routine from the moment you wake up.

For this reason I strongly recommend you do not attempt to give up while going to work. You really do need to spend a lot of time the first day keeping yourself relaxed and it would therefore be wise not to have much planned as you get used to managing your muscles again and unlearning the CNR. By the end of the second day the breath exercise on its own is all you will need to do for the majority of time with the occasional focus on the rest of your muscles.

Day two will be similar to day one with your muscles really starting to want to tense up. You may even notice them twitching as they attempt to tense up. Counter act this by focussing your mind on relaxing these sets of muscles and the twitching will stop.

The first two-day period is likely to be the most intense period of adaptation and will require lots of effort to stay relaxed. As long as you stay relaxed you will not think about wanting to consume nicotine at all. Remember if your muscles are relaxed you are telling your brain via the CNR that you are topped up with nicotine and don't want any more. Slowly but surely your brain is unlearning that nicotine is required to relax the muscles and your natural 'de-tensing' mechanism is starting to work again i.e. you taking positive action to relax yourself.

If you are quitting over the weekend then going to work on the Monday is achievable but you have to be very careful that you don't get caught out. By the third day your muscles will be two thirds the way there but will still need attention. It is very easy to think you are free from this drug and get caught out, believe me I've done it so many times there is no escaping the fact that you are still vulnerable for up to five days after you have stopped consuming as it takes this long to fully unlearn the CNR.

The first day requires the most effort but the amount of effort drops off as the days pass so much so that by the end of day three you really will think you have escaped the trap and to a large extent you have, as almost all the nicotine will be out of your body and if you've done things correctly you will have unlearned the CNR.

Days four and five though, still require you to keep on top of things and keep doing the breath exercise. You will feel that you don't need to, but your brain has only just unlearnt the CNR and you are vulnerable for this to still kick in and give you a fright.

It's as if your brain suddenly realises that it has been tricked from getting its usual fix and the CNR will suddenly trigger at the most unlikely time. For this reason, I include days four and five as part of the re-conditioning time period as you are definitely still vulnerable from a kind of rebound effect from the brain. It's as if it's saying to you 'are you sure you want to do this?' You just have to do the relax techniques to say to the brain 'yes I want this'.

Once you are through day five it should all be over, and you will only have to employ your relaxation techniques whenever you become naturally tense. If you don't you will just remain tense and agitated but you won't think about consuming nicotine to combat this as you have unlearned the CNR and so it can't trigger the brain to demand nicotine. You will just think I need to unwind somehow. The breath technique is very good for this and I would recommend never stop using it to stay relaxed.

CHAPTER 8

MOTIVATING YOURSELF TO STOP

Once you have become addicted to nicotine it can seem impossible to give up, no matter how hard you try. As a result, millions of people just accept nicotine addiction as part of their lives and give up trying to give up.

My method of getting off nicotine is totally unique and attacks the problem in such a way that means you will not experience any cravings whatsoever. In just 5 days you can be totally free of this drug forever. The secret is to unlearn the CNR. This is the key to long term success which is simply not addressed by any other method. All you need to do is that. It really is quite simple when it comes down to it.

I promise you though giving up nicotine is the most wonderful experience you can possibly have in your life. The longer you've been a consumer the more profound this experience will be. You will suddenly feel the most enormous burden lifted from you. A burden you had no idea you were carrying. It will hit you like a freight train and you will be sick to the stomach as you realise that you have been well and truly conned for so long.

You absolutely are being conned every waking minute of your life by nicotine. The whole purpose of nicotine is to trick you into giving away huge amounts of money. The people who are selling it to you know exactly how this drug works and consequently they don't consume it themselves. They are not that stupid; they know it doesn't do anything!

In my life as a smoker I used to smoke roughly 10 cigarettes a day during the week and then probably easily 30 on a weekend. That's on average 80 per week. When I smoked a pack of 20 was about £5. I worked out that I therefore spent over £10,000 in the 10 years that I smoked. How I managed that I do not know as I was at school and a student for a lot of that time. At today's prices though that would be £25k every 10 years!

Nicotine consumption is highest amongst the poorest people in our society. This is due to the fact that nicotine is perceived as a cheap way of getting a bit of pleasure in life rather than buying expensive clothes, cars and houses etc. We must start asking ourselves why this is so. Why is a drug that is so powerful, that doesn't actually give us the hit that we think it does, allowed to be sold to us at all? It makes no sense other than the fact that it is another way of getting money out of us.

You on the other hand have been brainwashed into believing that this drug actually does do something. Even now after everything I've been telling you about how this drug works, you are still probably doubting what I've said. That's how deep it goes!

You have to believe me when I tell you that this drug only makes you feel good after it has made you feel bad. On its own there is no lift. When you first consumed it there was no high. You didn't laugh or feel euphoric. Once you have properly got off nicotine, if you try it again it will make you feel sick and you will not want to consume it again, I guarantee it; but you have to get off it properly by unlearning the CNR.

When you first consumed nicotine you were coming to it with the belief that it did something. That's because you have grown up watching other people consuming it either in real life or on TV. We are all exposed to huge amounts of subliminal messaging and, as a consequence, up to the point of you first trying it, you have wondered all your life what all the fuss is about?

This has been reinforced by the fact that the law of the land means that it is seen as an adult only pleasure. Like alcohol you are only allowed to consume it once you have become old enough to 'know' what you are doing. It's something adults do and so as a child you can't wait to try!

The problem is no-one is being told the real truth about nicotine. We are told that people choose to smoke and it's their choice if they want to smoke. This is absolute lies. The companies selling this stuff know exactly that it is a simple physiological con trick and all they need to do is get you to try it. It's that powerful!

You will always hear that people choose to smoke. It's their choice. Yes, it is maybe their choice to try nicotine but they are blissfully unaware of what they are actually letting themselves in for. They have no idea that they are about to consume a mind-bending drug that will rewire their brains so quickly that they will begin to perceive consumption as pleasurable within just a few doses.

That's how quickly it works and that is one of the main reasons people are convinced it does actually give you pleasure. It's the first dose though that gives you the true effect, remember that. Remember that you had to try it more than once to see if there was a hit.

I remember trying my first cigarette and immediately afterwards wanted to try another one because I didn't feel any effects. It really makes me angry when I think back to how I kept trying to find the hit and of course eventually did. To say people choose to smoke is a blatant disregard of the fact that the majority of people who try it end up addicted to it. We choose to try it we do not choose to be brainwashed by it!

Also, we did not choose to become subliminally brainwashed by all the nicotine consumption that is shown on TV, which incidentally is supposed to be banned. The fact that people smoking is still allowed to be shown on TV should say it all. Yes, direct advertising is banned but the best advertising is just watching someone consuming it and showing that they are perceiving pleasure while they do so. This is the most powerful advertising there is. Direct advertising is all about brand loyalty but showing film stars smoking reinforces the ill-found public belief that nicotine gives you pleasure.

Why would people do it if it wasn't pleasurable? Because they have fallen for the world's biggest con that's why. No, they wouldn't choose to smoke if they knew the truth. But even when you know the truth once you're addicted it's so hard to stop. Until now!

Information about nicotine is not given to us. There is no-one telling you about the pharmacological effects of nicotine. Why are we not being told that it will take 3 days to get the majority of nicotine out of our bodies after just one dose? That's an awfully long time compared to other drugs. One unit of alcohol, for example, is broken down in only 1 hour!

There are no government sponsored adverts about nicotine even though it is responsible for millions of deaths every year. No, instead we are educated about all the illegal drugs. Does that not seem unusual? It does to me. Surely, out of all the drugs, we should be educated about the ones that we are legally allowed to take? The ones that we can clearly become addicted to. The ones that lead to millions of premature deaths every year! Are you trying to tell me that all the nicotine consumers out there are not addicted!

This is because they want you to become addicted. Both governments and the big corporations make too much money out of it. Let's talk about how much the UK government makes for starters. According to ASH (Action on Smoking and Health), in the financial year 2015-2016 the UK government made £9.5 Billion in revenue from cigarettes. That does not include VAT. The VAT collected on top of that would have been £2.4 Billion. In the same year it spent a mere £400,000 on quit smoking promotion and help programmes. Is there not room for a huge conflict of interests here? Why would any government want to give up that amount of revenue? Where's the incentive? Think about it, there is none.

Why would any government ever want to invest in schemes that would bring that amount of revenue down? They wouldn't. And who's bothered? It's not going to be a big vote winner as no-one really sees that the government should have a responsibility to do anything about it anyway. People 'choose' to smoke. So it's their funeral. We all believe people are making this choice. I did not choose to become addicted to nicotine and give £10,000 to cigarette companies, I can tell you that for sure!

Nicotine is a huge global business. Across the world 5 trillion cigarettes are consumed every year, that's 15 billion a day or 10 million every minute. 12% of the world's population are addicted to nicotine, that's 1.5 billion people. The world's largest tobacco company is based in China and makes 2.5 trillion cigarettes every year netting $170 billion dollars. That is just one cigarette company! Imagine the profits involved and the revenues governments are getting! Are you trying to tell me that this industry is free from corruption with this level of revenue?

As a result of the amount of money involved the truth will never be told and if governments are seen to be clamping down on nicotine it would be portrayed by the media that governments were taking away people's rights and freedom to choose what they want to do with their lives. That's how deep the rabbit hole goes. This thing is so big it has influence over every aspect of our lives to make sure the truth never gets out.

Nicotine catches so many people out. It is so subtle no-one sees it coming. When I started smoking just about everybody I knew who tried it ended up becoming addicted for many years. I only know of one person who tried it and didn't carry on with it out of about twenty other peers. One in twenty! We were like lambs to the slaughter. Living in an age when only two drugs are legally allowed to be consumed by adults just invites children to try it. Why wouldn't they, it's legal when you are old enough so it must be safe?

As children we are well and truly conditioned to look for pleasure from consuming things as we have been given sweets all our lives and nice foods as 'treats'. Putting something in our mouths to give us pleasure is well and truly part of our culture so it's only natural children are going to want to try nicotine.

How can a civilised society allow a substance that doesn't actually do anything become legal. And how can a civilised society ban so many other drugs that are nowhere near as addictive as nicotine but still allow nicotine to be sold.

Once you escape the nicotine trap properly, I promise you will see it for what it really is, a simple physiological trick which keeps you coming back for more, hopefully for the rest of your life. How is it legal for people to make money out of this drug? Because it makes people so much money and our society is extremely corrupt that's why!

As well as making money from legal revenue governments have been caught taking bribes from tobacco companies. Most recently, for example, in 2015 the BBC exposed British & American Tobacco (BAT) for bribing government officials in East African countries in an effort to undermine anti-smoking laws.

Imagine therefore how much of this went down in the early days of the tobacco industry. It would have been huge and we are still suffering a hangover from this with our draconian laws on this substance and what we are officially told about the drug.

If children were allowed to consume it as soon as they were born they would never begin to smoke. They would feel sick and not get any sort of hit whatsoever. The fact that they are not allowed to do it only serves over time to deepen the belief in their minds that there really is something in it. This then pushes them, when they do get the chance to try it, often in their teen years, that there must be something in it so that even though the first dose did absolutely nothing they keep trying, searching for the hit.

Of course, because the drug has acted on their muscles they immediately get a slight withdrawal reaction from their muscles which means that a subsequent dose of nicotine does actually have an effect. It's only slight to begin with but it is the start of the conditioning process and it doesn't take too many more doses before this is well and truly imprinted in their minds.

This process is so subtle no-one sees it coming. The withdrawal feelings to begin with are almost imperceptible but enough to begin the process of conditioning the brain to associate relieving muscle tension, no matter how slight, with consumption of nicotine. Over time this gets more and more pronounced generating a response in the brain and firmly establishing the CNR. Once the CNR is established it has to be properly unlearned or it will always be there capable of initiating the desire for nicotine. This is why so many people keep going back to nicotine even after many years away from it.

Using my method you unlearn the CNR as you come off the drug so that it is fully reversed within 5 days. That's it! Once you are through it you will never go back. You will never think about consuming nicotine again. You will be back to how you were before you ever tried it, never thinking about it. You will never miss those doses you currently think are so special, like after meals and after sex for example. Your mind will just not think about it because the thing driving your mind, the CNR, will have gone. This is what drives the desire for nicotine and like I say the more you consume the more often this alarm bell will ring which is why the thought of giving up nicotine is such a profound issue, for most consumers, because the alarm bell is ringing all the time, literally!

I know people who have smoked tobacco all their lives from when they were teens to their mid-fifties. That's 40 years of smoking. They have become so conditioned that they have forgotten that their minds used to work differently. They are also so worn down by their addiction that they have just accepted that they will consume it for the rest of their lives. They simply cannot see any way of beating it and have long given up trying to stop. This is where you are heading, it gets harder and harder to stop and that is because your tolerance goes up and up the longer you consume. As your tolerance goes up the amount of time needed between doses goes down and down until it is eventually zero and you have to be constantly consuming it as the CNR is constantly activated.

As a consequence, once you are at this level you never feel satisfied as your mind is constantly tormented with the need to keep consuming nicotine. If you can afford it you will become a chain smoker, if you can't afford it you will just get used to riding out the CNR as long as you can, meaning for your whole life your brain is in a stressed out state, never at peace.

Now remember before you started consuming nicotine. Can you remember that you never thought about it? You were happy in your life on a day to day level that you didn't need to consume nicotine. You never thought about it ever. Can you remember that? Please take time to remember; it's important to spend some time doing this because that state of mind you had before you first started consuming nicotine is what I'm aiming to get you back to.

Believe me if you give up using my method you will have a new lease of life. Your mind will be at peace once again and you will begin to enjoy simply living like you did before you became addicted. You will not need nicotine to get you through life anymore. I absolutely guarantee it!

Addicts have forgotten that 'normal' people never, ever, think about consuming nicotine. If you give up nicotine properly and unlearn the CNR you will never think about consuming it again. You will not look at other consumers and get a pang to have some nicotine, you will just feel sorry for them and it will be a lovely reminder of the fact that you have escaped it at last. You will not feel that you are missing out on something.

When you properly get off this drug you will never think about it again. I can guarantee that this is what will happen to you if you understand how this drug works and follow my instructions to the letter.

The biggest hurdle that you must overcome is believing that you will totally forget about nicotine and that you will get back to feeling great on a day to day basis without ever thinking about consuming it. You will not miss nicotine one bit, on the contrary you'll be elated to have escaped its clutches!

Because the conditioning is so deep it is the fear that life without it will be miserable or boring that keeps addicts consuming. They are scared that if they give up they will be tormented every day by not being able to have that little hit. They are convinced that life will not be the same without that lovely drug. How will they get up in the morning, I'm bound to miss that first one? And what about after a big meal, how can life be any good without a dose then?

This is where I need you to have absolute faith in my method. You will never want to consume nicotine again once you quit this way. You will hate it with a passion and you will be so angry that you let yourself be so conned for so long. You have to remember that first dose of nicotine and how it didn't do anything. This is your body's natural reaction to nicotine. It is a horrible habit and I will make you see that again. The addicted mind is shutting out the normal reaction as it needs nicotine regularly to avoid the uncomfortable withdrawal process.

Remember, there is no real hit, nicotine is just taking us from a below par state to a normal state and this lift is what we perceive as the hit. The more below par we are the better this 'hit' will be. All nicotine ever does is make us feel normal. How many consumers do you see with big smiles on their faces? None, because there is nothing that makes you feel better than normal. It is like holding in a wee. The pain builds up and up so much that it can feel great when you finally relieve yourself. This is just like nicotine. With this drug you are giving yourself a substance that will make you feel bad when you don't consume it for a while so that you get a hit when you consume it again. The longer you go in between hits the greater this potential perceived hit will be – it's as simple as that!

If you give up the right way you will stop thinking about nicotine immediately. Once and for all you will have beaten this thing that has had such a hold over every waking moment of your life. You will finally see how your brain has been in one constant state of withdrawal since you first started, and it has just been a relentless battle to keep the pangs at bay ever since. Get your life back and get off this drug once and for all. I promise, you will never look back. Good luck!

Printed in Great Britain
by Amazon

12280546R00031